Gardening Secrets of the Dead

Gardening Secrets of the Dead

Lee Herrick

WordTech Editions

Published by WordTech Editions
P.O. Box 541106
Cincinnati, OH 45254-1106

ISBN: 9781936370979
LCCN: 2012952132

Poetry Editor: Kevin Walzer
Business Editor: Lori Jareo

Cover Art, "The Weight of Forgiveness," by JooYoung
    Choi
Cover Design by Lisa Lee
Author Photo by Joel Pickford

Visit us on the web at www.wordtechweb.com

The author would like to extend his deepest gratitude to the editors of the following publications, where these poems previously appeared, sometimes in slightly different versions:

"Gardening Secrets of the Dead," *The Packinghouse Review*
"Freedom," *More Than Soil, More Than Sky: The Modesto Poets*
"Korean Poet in California," *One for the Money: The Sentence as Poetic Form*
"Kwi Ch'on," *Journal of Korean Adoption Studies*
"My California," *ZYZZYVA*
"Self-Portrait," *Mascara Literary Review*
"Spectral Questions of the Body" and "If We Are What We Eat," *Cha*
"Stars" was displayed in *Born Into Identity: The Asian Adoptee Experience* at the Wing Luke Asian American Arts Museum in Seattle, Washington
"Van Gogh Writes to Gauguin" and "Focus Theory," *Pebble Lake Review*

For Suzhen

Contents

1.

Korean Poet in California

I am one of the war fractures—
a breathing fact of art,

the artifice, the brass hiss
from Isang Yun's first exiled concerto—

touch my arms and you will know.

My California

Here, an olive votive keeps the sunset lit,
the Korean twenty-somethings talk about hyphens,

graduate school and good pot. A group of four at a window
table in Carpinteria discuss the quality of wines in Napa Valley
    versus Lodi.

Here, in my California, the streets remember the Chicano
poet whose songs still bank off Fresno's beer soaked gutters

and almond trees in partial blossom. Here, in my California
we fish out long noodles from the pho with such accuracy

you'd know we'd done this before. In Fresno, the bullets
tire of themselves and begin to pray five times a day.

In Fresno, we hope for less of the police state and more of a
    state of grace.
In my California, you can watch the sun go down

like in your California, on the ledge of the pregnant
twenty-second century, the one with a bounty of peaches
    and grapes,

red onions and the good salsa, wine and chapchae.
Here, in my California, paperbacks are free,

farmer's markets are twenty four hours a day and
always packed, the trees and water have no nails in them,

the priests eat well, the homeless eat well.
Here, in my California, everywhere is Chinatown,

everywhere is K-Town, everywhere is Armeniatown,
everywhere a Little Italy. Less confederacy.

No internment in the Valley.
Better history texts for the juniors.

In my California, free sounds and free touch.
    Free questions, free answers.
Free songs from parents and poets, those hopeful
    bodies of light.

Gardening Secrets of the Dead

When the light pivots, hum — not so loud
the basil will know, but enough
to water it with your breath.
Gardening has nothing to do with names
like *lily* or *daisy*. It is about verbs like *uproot*,
traverse, hush. We can say it has aspects of memory
and prayer, but mostly it is about refraction and absence,
the dead long gone when the plant goes in. A part of the body.
Water and movement, attention and dirt.

Once, I swam off the coast of Belize and pulled
seven local kids along in the shallow Caribbean,
their brown bodies in the blue water behind me,
the first one holding my left hand like a root,
the last one dangling his arm under the water
like a lavender twig or a flag in light wind.
A dead woman told me: Gardening,
simply, is laughing and swimming
a chorus of little brown miracles
in water so clear you can see yourself
and your own brown hands becoming clean.

Rhyme

If all the words in the world
rhyme, then

oranges taste like being alive,
ascent rhymes

with stop here, please
the grace of exiting rhymes

with the drunk pissing
The scarf rhymes

with the cost
no idea how

an hour moves this slow.

All we want is to not be watched.
All the glitches hiss.

Medicate. Meditate.
Korea, homeland. Go quietly

then resist
how perfect you are, this time

Pho

Praise be to the lovers who devour
fall's luscious onions and lime,
the broth and noodles perfect each time
they wonder how to best spend a free hour—
with sprouts, Sriracha and Buddha admiring our
bliss, the music, the grandmothers, the rhyme
from the kitchen, the young chicken in its prime
hacked up last night before we lost power.

        Look. Some dishes are holy.
And some are just dishes.
I have been to Viet Nam, Hue
in mid-morning when the boats depart slowly.
I will eat what pho the good woman wishes.
Come along with us. Let us eat once we pray.

Why I Travel

Because Frida painted spines and blues
Because I wanted to learn the velocity of malaise
Because I needed to sit in Lima's sloping plazas
Because I was born in Korea and raised
in the Bay Area's hills and Modesto's orchard acoustics
Because the valley wants you to and the city wants you to
Because wars unfold into other little wars
and I saw how some bombs detonate on your very own bridge
Because I saw the Salvadoran woman shape the pupusa
and her daughter shaping God's face on the comal
Because your voice on the other side of the world
still sounds like your voice
Because the Great Wall may well stun you
Because the Mekong River may well stun you
Because Lake Calhoun may well stun you
Because Qingdao's beach may stun you
Because El Paso's writers may stun you
Because the birds in my city may well stun you

If We Are What We Eat

I am the raw jellied crab
in a small room in Insadong

I am pork browning on the barbecue
the lavender bud under the tongue

I am you and not you, the document
of black ink and number sequences

I am stacks of ham
and the dead scorpion in Beijing

the squid in Incheon, all the blossoms
from the tree in full bloom,

the trees and the bark, the wood
fire, the cold beer,

the fish I want to be but cannot be,
how I am not myself

but I am my skin, my hair,
slivers of black moon like ice.

On the Bank of the Mekong

Sunset in Laos is an open document,
a bike tire rut in the mud, a flower
from the market and the lettuce rolls,
the kid you kick the soccer ball with
and his father who comes to wonder
who you are, the fresh French bread,
a residual delight from the occupation,
the Vietnamese neighbors gawking
about tanks and fitted suits.
It is like that wind at the young man's
back as he weaves past the defender
with a step over, not even breaking stride,
not caring about his neighbor tearing
at his only Brazil jersey, not caring that
the weather next month will damage the rice
and cause trouble with the one following that.

Outside the Front Window at Home

At last, the pigeon strolls to the window
by the sidewalk and eats. It is smaller
than the pigeons in La Paz as far as
I can tell. The angered squirrel
clasps her claws and realizes the world
is not hers, nor are these seeds I've thrown
before the grass. The pigeon is a study
in balance—one wing raised and torn,
one wing tucked and blue.

Grace

"Grace is an arrow shot through the air."
—Tina Chang

Once, I thought danger was everywhere
one went, slippery inescapable canal banks
surrounded by killer Doberman pinchers
with teeth like knives and bad stories.
After this many sunsets,
I learned I was only surrounded by grace,
yours each time you told me *no*,
you with a full basket of arrows and warning signs
you, not a path of cliffs but the ascension,
you, so much light the whole room glowed,
you, like this room, with new light and angels.

Poetry

Daedumi on the dress,
smoke from silk worms

on the grill
winds into the lamp and vanishes.

In Itaewon,
Sunday morning, drunk kids

in fine black clothes spill and stumble
down the street

toward Hangjing station.
Climb the steps to Namsan and take

a view of the city. Hee Won teaches

today about American culture.
She asks me to guest lecture.

But all I can imagine is red jujube tea,
tangerine peels, raspberry

wine, its sweet dark pursed lips.

Desire

All the city wanted it got: clean
blue water in a pool
circular gathering places
sloped east for drainage
& parade routes.

The plaza should be small
enough for children,
large enough for muralists' Sunday
dreaming oils, canvas, affairs.

In order to love yourself
you need only sing
in the center of the plaza
and kneel in blue water.

Everything else means trouble.
Think about Him. Yours sins
are his. This is a nail &
you are not dying.

Orchestral

The intricate pretensions speak
a singular language in code, hidden
pings and choral patterns
for the enthusiastic front row
awed by the conductor's
unexpected sense of humor.

How choreographed, his right
hand on her shoulder as the violins
took position and all the formal attire
the perfect accompaniment
to the seduction, the nice wine,
the rice paper invitations
in turn of the century
Beijing impressions.

For this sort of drama
more generations are needed—
toddlers for levity and symbol,
great-grandparents for perspective,
gravity. Dress them in black, too.
Drape everyone in the Western
tradition of imperialist, lover.
Let the conductor's whiskey
breath slide because the war
has ended and the sons and
daughters are coming home.

2.

Fire

This is death and air
the absence of sufficient prayer

the self-immolation of Thich Quang Duc in Ho Chi Minh

City, doused in gasoline,
then the match, the wind, the air, the smoke, the fire.

This is the soul's whistling
over the Vietnamese rooftops, over the fathers and daughters

over the singed and the poor.
This is about campfires, suburban fires made by husbands

nearly dead or the soldier
poet with the fire inside,
the pyromaniac down
the block, and the Bolivian
student on the cusp of her
own little revolution.

Some fires take a long time to blossom.
Chances are high you will not even notice the smoke.

Once, I broke down on the couch.

I thought I was going to die.

This is different than the time I broke down

        in front of my father at nineteen because
I did not want to die. My father saved me that night.

What if the dead knew about each of our dreams?
What if they forgave you?
What if we knew the secrets of all the city's acoustics?
Would it matter if I told you I know nothing,
that there is no thing I want to tell you more than
how much I have fallen in love with this world,

all of its fires, its failures, its faith,
how I love all of your past fires, now ash?

Beach Dreams

I pick up all the pieces and make an island / Might even raise a little sand.

Jimi Hendrix, "Voodoo Child"

In the grove, there were three birds like a choir.
In the alley, cat after cat like drunks from the bar.
In the dream, the guitarist's solo face in a mural.
Gather all the pieces into your favorite bag.
Gather the neglected granules and seek out birds.
In the birds, a choir of murals and sand.
In the bar, the guitarist dreams about the valley.
In the sand, carve the name of the woman you love.

Kwi Ch'on

for Ch'on Sang Pyong, 1930—1993

Because after imprisonment, you could laugh
with your mouth so wide open, as if to swallow
the swirling bats of the CIA, because when you
disappeared in 1971, your friends thought
about your poems and you going back to heaven,
because I am dreaming of the sunset over Eurwangni
tonight, there is jujube tea in Insadong waiting for us.
Did you drink every hour of 1972?
And when they found you, unable
to remember your name but that you were a poet,
did you remember the answer to your own question?
That there is no answer at all but the request that
someone would find you in that fractured slur,
the tired lean and the pen your only possession,
that someone like her, with a language like food,
would know how tea can restore such fatigue?

Dear Prisoner

In your dark cell, imagine
Ko Un's quiet face

during his imprisoned years, when—
to pass the time and salvage sanity—

he imagined the face of every person
he ever met,

brought their gestures,

the monks' contentment,
the ghosts and lovers

before love, the Korean man's joy
unleashed after his country scores

a goal. Imagine privacy, privilege,
each brown face an undiscovered country.

The Novelist Dies in a Remote Train Station

"How do peasants die?"

— Leo Tolstoy

If there were a treasure map
in the gasping peasant's pocket,

he would not die in an abandoned house
full of pristine first editions

I have left you
the contents of my pockets—

crushed leaves, a good pen,
some money.

Air,
said the drunk,

is the least of his concerns.
He is concerned about shadows

at the wrong angles
and the unspoken apologies.

He cares, you know.
He cares about these crushed leaves.

I am glad the air was so clean
on the night of his death.

I am glad his questions formed wings
and flew into their own little heavens.

Dear You

I am in the third draft of my first novel
that asks *what if I had been in an orphanage
in the south instead of here in Pyongyang,*
where we have beautiful dancers but no mail?
The protagonist has become an unruly
punk with far too many questions.

So I am taking a break.
I write you from The Shifting Northern Limit Line.
I want to send a letter. I want to open mail
from an imaginary friend, a writer in New York City.
I want to explain the third draft's opening,
where a young couple walks along the beach
and comes to a bunker, the barbed wire and sandbags,
the sand and shells that envelop the denouement.
Should I bring in The Cheonan, another 46 dead
like the 115 dead from the downed plane a few years back?
What do those little kids do in the orphanages?
The older ones who have left will return and take pictures
with the new kids and they will figure out their own ways
to navigate this kind of separation—

some will paint, some will dance
some will wince, some will wind
their energies into an intricate

novel plot or write a letter about beautiful dancers whose grace could make you forget your name.

Light

for Julia Ji Hye Mendelson, 1982-2007

How light is your room in Jerusalem?
If love is air, then you breathe it into the world—

to Amie in California, who thinks of you tonight,
to Frederik, born in Rwanda and adopted to Belgium at 8,

he thinks of your laughter. And Laura, who wanted
     to embrace you
in Philadelphia. She is here, too.

I wonder, Julia, how light are you tonight?
On the subway in Seoul, when you fell asleep

in 2005 before the blasts and the chemo,
did you know your light could outweigh even this?

I don't know what light I have—but here it is. Take it.

The Sudanese mother to whom you teach Hebrew,

you are her light.

All the adoptees in Copenhagen, New York, Seoul,
we share light, don't we? And yours,

the shining want, the Grace you embody,
is a lamp in us. Take these lamps and sleep.

And then, wake again and breathe.

Four Deaths

1

The little shatter

indiscernible from the grand dying

around it

2

Her knowing.

Call it the first real break.

Staring at the clouds'

mercy for hours.

3

Rebirth and season

of writing after the second death.

That first shatter now soil,

half submerged.

4

The elegant seduction

from gravity. Tell me a story before I die.

At times like this, I wish you were in the room.

Van Gogh Writes to Gauguin

When Van Gogh
wrote the letter to his friend, Gauguin,
and told him that he had felt well as of late,
that he had been painting olive trees with which he was pleased,
I want to know if he thought about death in that letter
and if death by his own hand was stirred away by those paints
in his hand, as now, I am trying not to think about death,
not by my own hand, but by my own disregard
for this abundant stillness, the calm sound in the center
of my stomach. They were oils, Van Gogh's olive trees.
And if the canvas could speak, it might choose not to.
It knew about genius and the madness involved with the trees,
the olives dancing on the branches like grenades.

3.

Stars

Imagine the stars. And the birth fathers. The birth mothers.
The parents. The agencies and prophecies. How each star lights
the roots in the ground, the routes on the roads.

Imagine your birth mother's body was taken
over by tuberculosis or other forms of dying—
lack of water, hope, or infrastructure.

You may go back. You may speak with the police.
Kind translators. You may go on live national television
or go on via webcam from Sydney, Copenhagen, or St. Paul.

The Korean television hosts, gorgeous.
You may search but in fact there may no one searching
for you. There may someone missing you or trying not to miss you.

There may be someone who hides from you.
(There are ways to manage this tangled grace
where a North American couple adopts a Korean boy

the same day you visit Holt to get your adoption file.
There may be no more information than what a half-sleeping
policeman's best effort can muster, how they will tell you

Kim Kyeop Gol is dead, how Shim Soon Duk is now
with Parkinson's and does not remember taking care of you.
But you find new love when you go digging. You will find

a woman named Lim Hyo-in, graceful and sixty in Daejeon,
helping you search. You will meet a gracious woman
named Choi Eun-Seong and she will translate for you,

looking into the television camera, as you say, half-trembling,
I was born in Daejeon in December 1970.
My birth name is Lee Kwang Soo. My Korean age is 39.)

You will talk about peace, about love, how you want to feel
your birth mother's hand on your chest. You will not say
you want to cry and then be quiet for weeks.

You want to tell them what they already know,
that you thought of them in every city,
how you speak with ghosts in every city.

And what about your birth father?
Do you have a sister in this world?
Do they shudder the same way you do?

Do all the stars in the sky amount to anything?
If they all had a moment of common language,
would they even come to realize they are stars?

Gathering

Here, tonight, as we gather
our stray and common
ideas, our blossoming flowers
in the shapes of wine glasses

an Asian father thinks of you in a beautiful gallery
and admires the texture of your black hair,
grateful to unite with friends whose laughter perfumes
the air like memories you store at home.

Tonight, we resemble
a beautiful painting,
don't we?

We celebrate and assemble
from around the world,
around how good it feels to be free
to be the anger and or the grace,
to discover more of yourself
how you are the light, the smile,
the flower in the grand bouquet.

Circle

for Jennifer and Sun Yung Shin

Once, I thought I had memory,
browned dry leaves in a pile,

Korean, full of smoke,
autobiography as division:

north of the Han River, south of it
the 63 Building, a gold rocket

all the red neon crucifixes lit
under Seoul's hopeful twilight

the Imjing River's heavy bloat,
the guardposts with handprints

of former soldiers like my translator
who helped me try to find my birth mother.

You write about paper and savagery:
all the dying and flowers to the left
all the dying and flowers to the right
all the children eating popsicles to the left
all the children eating popsicles to the right

Your shattering elegance

you graceful astronomy
you turn into doves,
you sword of fire through the snow
we will remember it all.

Exile

Transit to the new country
study the preamble and the periodic
table of elements, laugh at the racist jokes,
become American, then undo what you've
learned and become human.
We do not know much of the prologue here.
I landed in the United States on October 12, 1971.
What we know is this: x minus y
predicates belief in these letters
in the first place, some certainty
or concern for extra credit.
I do not commit to your math.
I have almost freed myself of the verb *want*.
To desire is to lose sight of everything.
I care only about food and digression,
that half cup of water
that could keep you alive for weeks.

Self-Portrait

I am twenty-five yards past the last breaking wave
a flute plateaued at the maestro's steady baton hand
I am five stones from the last good wind

I am four bones from a cow after the shotgun.
I am the idea that did not detonate.

Brothers, we are Korean, so we know
about fracture – family, country, tongue.
We know the volcanic descent of government.

Once, a woman told me
I am the only one who understands
the cost of her survival.

So we did all we could.
We touched each other's hands,
inhaled deeply, contemplated not letting go.

Portrait of the Korean Adoptee with Partial Alphabet

Air

A propeller swats through your chest when you think of her.
I landed in San Francisco, from Seoul, on October 12, 1971.
There was not a parade.

Birth Name

Could have been a cop, could have been an employee,
could have been my birth mother who named me: Lee Kwang
    Soo.

Cucumber kimchi

Please pass the cucumber kimchi. Please, the lemon soju.
Please, the blotted history.
Meat will keep you happy. You will think of me when you get
hungry.

Demographics

He fails math when stories are introduced, begins to care less
about numbers and more about arcs, shadows, plots, and lies.

Daejeon

Outside the Express Train Station, in May, there are blooms

so light they could evaporate. You should go there to find out
  for yourself.

Dae-Won

He speaks *five* languages. We had beer and dried squid near
  KoRoot.
He is angel. Some kind of work is just holy.

Etymology

Eulogy. Egg. The world-wide wasted elegies.

Father

GOA'L

Good luck, good times, good boy, good banchan.

Holt

Imjing River. In Daejeon, we almost got lost.

Jennifer Kwon Dobbs, Jane Jeong Trenka. Some kind of
  art is this pure.

KBS

KoRoot

Lee Kwang Soo is my birth name. I am 39. I will not go on.

May 6, 2008, I discovered I was born in or near Daejeon.

Nomenclature

Nam Dae Mun is not on fire in my dream. There is no smoke.
9143 is my Holt case number. You should see my photo.
    I was plump and shocked.

Shim Soon-Duk . Sun Yung Shin.

T
U
V

When one sense fails you, the other five will save your
    life.

X, ex, axes, axis. We are not evil.

You

You piece together what you can, when you can.
In the meantime, breathe as if your chest is an ocean.

Spectral Questions of the Body

When I imagine my birth mother's body, spectral
questions float: how the cage
of bone protects the heart, how she sounded
near death once or if bird cried
a song near the river. I imagine it like gel
in a body of water, a jellyfish in the sea,
a gasping squid.

                            If I could touch the body,
I would go for the neck
where air meets air, despair swapped for light
flashes, cusps of cut lavender,
cups of the silkworms you may have loved,
the new breathing.

                        This is how I imagine

your body: brown and surfacing, a changing shape
of grace and light to mirror
the foreboding chant of my own death,
or the true loss of a child in Korea
who goes West to become a child in America,
full of spectral images distracting him from
all the Korean trees, the clashing bodies,
all the animals and angels calling out his name.

Border

I want to walk the four kilometers
from end to end,
where Panmunjom begins and the crying is
a deep river you will not cross.
You will not cry when the father goes to the north
and you will never see him again
unless you die, arm yourself, or escape.
What have you ever escaped?
What have you ever found and kept?
What guns can you possibly tell me about?

Korea

It was a flower on fire, a fugue
lit by the maestro's thin bow

scraping its heat against the string.
Things ignite after a while.

Ask your father. Ignition does
not always flame, though, as we know

wind is required, or at least sufficient oxygen.
I can't remember much of anything

except Mike asking me if I have ever eaten dog,
Roy with the camera on his shoulder,

Hoya trying her best. There was Lim,
that anthology of grace,

Eun-Seong, her translations
from English into Korean and back again,

the way she was one of us, the ones whose lives
scrape back together

to find ample oxygen
to flame, flower, fugue.

Document

Here, a black pen for memory. There, stacks of galbi.
Here, a green scarf with ample gallantry.

The city opened itself, so what else could we do
but dive in and swim? Let's sip this and trace

all the apostrophes back to their villages,
this hospital gone, the name of that orphanage

misspelled, the date of birth you once craved,
how we become someone's ideograph.

We are no longer children. We are the new roots.
We can float like you would not believe.

Born

I was born in an ocean of poor magic
near a songwriter with stories

but no maps, strung out
on local wine and rice.

I was born because the magic and the birds
were certain they'd seen me before.

There were no gasps or hands
clapping nor arias or sobs. I was there

on the grass, a full head of black hair,
eyes that asked, *will you say a little more*

a curiosity that became desire,
then death, then desire again.

4.

April

You gift of ideas and peril, clean swells
and vows to remember how a three month old
elephant seal crawls onto the beach toward
the rocks, he has not eaten in a month
barely able to curl and growl at the beach
dog wanting to sniff.

You gift of rage and lilacs, the government
dogs scraping the people's bones
for meat and tax fat.
You gift of city thugs,
drunk kids howling out of tune,
you beautiful occasion

April, your ease, the wind, the pelicans,
the clean sand, the elephant seal saved
so he can do what seals do, dive a mile
deep, hold his breath underwater
for an hour, swim from Santa Barbara
to Hawai'i and then once per year, return home—

for mating, for memory, for moving
again to a new beach, where a man will
walk the wide sand and find another seal,
helpless and tired. The man will lean down
over it and pray. The seal will not understand
the man's prayers, but he will survive.
He may forget what month it was but he will
remember the sound of that prayer.

Elegance

If elegance matters here,
the vases ought to keep

their flowers in order.

The piano and bourbon

should shock up into the sky
like a team of seagulls.

The end will not come

sooner or noticeably so

if we let the lawn crawl
over the pavement

just so, let the hair crawl

over the ear just so,

let the vases gather water
stains and harden. Will it?

Will making space

in the day for thinking of snow

and tattoos bring anything closer
or keep the good music at bay?

Will this repair even matter?

Is this a repair at all?

Who says violins aren't
playing this very moment?

Elation

You *can* be several places at once:
literally, on earth, in North America,

in California, in a plastic white lawn chair
on the porch, the rain not sure what it wants

to perform, an aria or a fury, you are there,
in the white chair, the plastic cardinal's

spinning wings gauging the wind, and then you
become the two birds that flew

into the luncheon while the fiction speaker talked
about rooms in Buenos Aires.

One of the birds landed on the chair next to me.
It was a dove.

All this, and you imagine what dreams
your daughter's nap brings:

racing down the sidewalk on her new pink scooter,
noticing each fallen leaf, on the lookout for cats.

You imagine the texture of the poet's hair,
how each strand flares in the light rain.

And there is something else you didn't know—
the dead butterflies? I saved all of their wings.

I told you I would.

2008

He is not in love with the air
sucked through

clenched teeth or the fluted air,
blown slowly

through a mouthful of damp leaves.
Not in love

with the brunette's *come here
and talk to me* smile

It was a difficult year.

He imagines his face
a small brittle leaf and shatters it

in his open, vacant palms.

As It Begins

A batch of yellow daisies strung
by a light blue yarn, tossed on the beach
by lovers gone to make love in the room.
There are rocks to watch out for
as with most beaches in dreams.
But he focuses on her waist,
her lips moving separately from the words,
you know, we should have another one.
There's the bar and the bourbon,
a cell phone the drunk left behind,
the ringtone *Smoke on the Water,*
her lean, her hand through the end
of her black hair, the pianist
who knows just what song to play.

Scene from an Imaginary Film

The lobby so palatial and vacant
except our thawing bodies on the couch,
curled against each other as if the world
were just our tongues and hands, we slept
in different rooms across the city and somehow
kept our stories to ourselves. We will call
this a third space, floating. Or attraction.
Or how we burrowed our palms into each
other's palms, how culture seeped
in, as it always will.
                                     I almost fell in love
with you and your dead. I am here, an echo
and a black glimpse. I know what you mean,
your angelic map, your black hair wave above
this room full of bodies. We let go
our dead and try to sleep ourselves clean.

The Body

If the body is just flakes and shells, leaves
and one good trunk for the planting—

if it amounts to what one timely prayer can absolve,
if it matters to you—

Have you noticed the body's questions?
You did, after all, stay up

until the sun rose that morning
when you thought you couldn't make it,

like now, when you thought you couldn't make it.
You have what amounts to one prayer left.

No. You have thousands left.
But your body wants the same

as the last body you touched.
It wants to forget itself,

as it stains the skin without apology,
as it goes like verse through the blood.

Focus Theory

The black hair
the sweat on your neck,
the everlasting question.
Her lips on the wine glass.
Imagine all the beaches.
The curve of her hip.
More piano, more wind through the hair.

Once, I sang as if I were a small choir,
its voice indiscernible from the fire next door,
the birth of a boy right on time.

He is blessed now
with good luck and rice, balancing
on various borders for the rest of his life:
north and south
east and west
mother and mother.

Music will mitigate whatever you want.
The acoustic chord is a simple sound.
When I go to the next world,

I want one clear moment of focus.
I want lavender and waves. There had better be waves.
I want to hear you, repeating over and over,

if one sense fails you,
the other five will save your life.

Field

She asked me to explore
with her, so we

drove as far the dirt road would take us
she said, *look,*

a country road
but I didn't point out the sign that said

this is not a country road

her purple dress alight
on her body, we sat on my Jeep's hood

she pointed out constellations
we created new ones with strange names

she named each bird as it sang
its brilliant whistle

past the moon and its hope

this is a field in America
here is where I fell in love

Chorus

The holes in the flute can be covered,
as can the gaps in the heart.

We are a chorus, you and I—
grandparents' echoing bird voices

like cymbals and accents,
God's singular *yes*

like a last sea blow
after months on dry land.

And what can be said about the ocean?
The slow wash onto the beach is pitch

on each time, and the music
of your starry body, the water's diamonds

gather in your hair—your laughter
a palette, our own drum solo

and rattle, the snare only now,
the birds go into their jazz again.

North America

I never wanted to taste your beach
sand as a baby, watching the ommas
waving goodbye to the bus driver in Itaewon.
I never wanted your lights like I want them now,
swirled in mid-grade bourbon, glistening
reminders of *yes*, the word I hiss when
I think of North America from Central America,
Tacuba to be exact, the narrow street
by the grade school where the Americas blur.

America, I fell in love with one of yours,
a Hmong American woman who speaks
French and Mandarin and makes moussaka
as if she were an old Greek woman.
America, this is why I am in love with you:
Kelly's chickens in Olema, the cows
on the Tomales Bay Trail,
the quiet afternoons in Fresno,
the light the bay lets off,
our Asian America, our banchan,
our city of constellations,
our stories, our story,
our bone echo.

The Impossible Replication of Desire

How much delight before we collapse
How much earth in the lungs
How much wine

When we want more
When the weeds sprawl
It is not what you think

Think how fast some landscapes change
the lover, the gardener's grand idea,
the failing Maple

the boat about to capsize
the correction
the hand's reflection

the impossibile replication of weight
versus time
how it will never mean what you want

Truth

"The truth has propellers that find canals to beat in your
chest."

—Kevin A. Gonzalez

The truth is not the cage
nor the heart, nor lungs

but the momentum, some song
you loft at a cloud one day.

It is God
and light in your laughter, daughter.

Equations evolve.
You should know this, love.

You should know how
I dream of your heart.

The Heart

Let us remember the heart.
You can stir it up or stone it up,
carve out a moat to blockade it
with murky water and little alligators
to protect it, or invent stories
with limping villains who scratch
their names into its chambers
and assign natives the blame.
You can pray to reshape it or
re-imagine it as an open hand.

What if it could atrophy or implode?
What about xenograft?
The butterfly's long chambered heart
forms after the chrysalis splits.
The little beauty lives for only
two weeks, so its heart would not do
or maybe you would take flight.
What about the heart's ambition,
the drunk pianist's secret love
arranged near the tall vase?

Imagine Christian Barnard's hands.
He performed the first heart transplant
in 1967. Imagine the size of Kelly Perkins'
new heart, when she scaled Mount Kilimanjaro
with it. Take yours and its aspirations,

what it wants to scale or embrace.
Let us remember the heart beats
thirty five million times per year,
the size of a child's fist, a child's
question, once around the sun.

Spar, reunite—take truth, death, faith,
and myth—mix with water and patience.
I apologize for my imperfections' open mouths
touting their little slogans in the moonlight,
but not for my heart's little beating
into the morning hours, a pulse, a mountain,
but mostly I do not apologize for my heart's
late surfacing, its perfect missing chunk
from the upper chamber that takes five years
to properly close and then, once more, open.

Freedom

Logic suspends it for only so long, given fire,
given water. If we were more

elemental and less of the mind,
you could imagine the problems—skin,

revealed for what it is, less than what
we aspire to, given angels, given sky.

Look. Start over. We have
the open architecture for such capacity,

a new line, a real shift.
Do not let the roof or the net keep you from it.

Do not let that voice that sounds like your voice
keep you from it. It is beyond that,

outside of your body,
aloft and everywhere you are.

About the Author

Lee Herrick is the author of *This Many Miles from Desire*
(WordTech Editions, 2007). His poems have appeared in literary
journals such as *ZYZZYVA, Many Mountains Moving, The
Bloomsbury Review, Hawai'i Pacific Revie*w, and *From the
Fishhouse* online, among others, and in anthologies such as *Seeds
from a Silent Tree: Writings by Korean Adoptees, Highway 99: A
Literary Journey Through California's Great Central Valley*, 2nd
Edition, *The Place That Inhabits Us: Poems from the San
Francisco Bay Watershed*, and *One for the Money: The Sentence
as Poetic Form*. He is the founding editor of *In the Grove* and
Guest Editor of *New Truths: Writing in the 21st Century by
Korean Adoptees* for Asian American Poetry and Writing. He
teaches at Fresno City College in Fresno, California and in the
low-residency MFA Program at Sierra Nevada College.